MATH CODES FOR MINECRAFTERS

SKILL-BUILDING PUZZLES AND GAMES FOR HOURS OF ENTERTAINMENT!

JEN FUNK WEBER

Copyright © 2020 by Hollan Publishing, Inc.

Minecraft® is a registered trademark of Notch Development AB.

The Minecraft game is copyright © Mojang AB.

Sky Pony Press books may be purchased in bulk at special discounts for sales promotion, corporate gifts, fund-raising, or educational purposes. Special editions can also be created to specifications. For details, contact the Special Sales Department, Sky Pony Press, 307 West 36th Street, 11th Floor, New York, NY 10018 or info@skyhorsepublishing.com.

Sky Pony® is a registered trademark of Skyhorse Publishing, Inc.®, a Delaware corporation.

Visit our website at www.skyponypress.com.

10 9 8 7 6 5 4

Library of Congress Cataloging-in-Publication Data is available on file.

Cover design by Brian Peterson

Cover and interior illustrations by Amanda Brack

Book design by Kevin Baier

Math codes created by Jen Funk Weber

Print ISBN: 978-1-5107-4724-1

Printed in China

MATH CODES FOR
MINECRAFTERS

TABLE OF CONTENTS

A PRICKLY SUBJECT

Find the sums of the math problems, then use the code-breaker key to reveal the answer to the joke.

24	25	26	27	28	29	30	31	32	33	34	35	36	37	38
A	B	C	D	E	F	G	H	I	J	K	L	M	N	O

39	40	41	42	43	44	45	46	47	48	49
P	Q	R	S	T	U	V	W	X	Y	Z

What would you get if you could breed a pig with a cactus in the Desert biome?

16 + 8	27 + 12	13 + 25	34 + 7	25 + 9	22 + 26
24					

17 + 25	14 + 25	24 + 8	26 + 11	19 + 9

A _ _ _ _ _ _ _ _ _ _ _

IN THE BALANCE

Time to rack up some experience!

The first scale is balanced. You must balance the second scale before it tips, lands on the pressure plate, and launches a hidden arrow right at you!

How many  do you need to balance the second scale? Draw them or write the number on the scale.

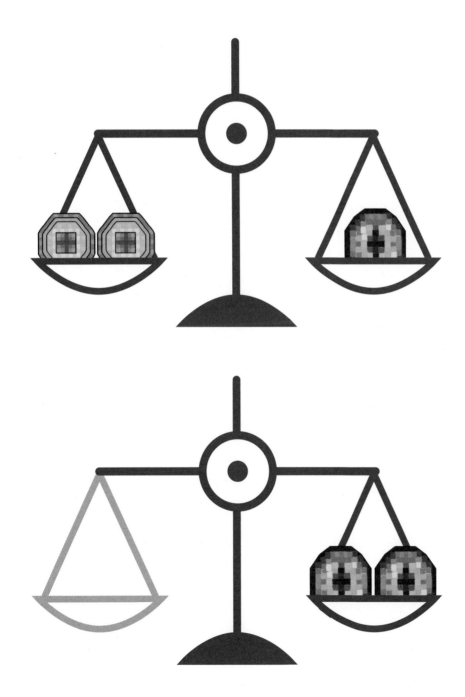

HILARIOUS HAUNT

Move from box to box as you count by fours. Write the letter from each box where you land on the spaces, in order from left to right. Begin with the number 4 and continue until all the spaces are filled. If you count, hop, and copy letters correctly, you'll reveal the answer to this question:

What might you call a tamed wolf that comes back from the dead?

14
 	
A
    24
	16
	
	B
	44
		36
		
		E
		    20

22
 	
O
    8
	28
	
	G
	    34
		④
		
		Z
		10

18 **M** 12	26 **R** 30	40 **L** 32

Z __ __ __ __ __ __ __ __

MAGIC NUMBER 1

The numbers at the end of the rows are linked to the images in the grid. What number goes in the circle? This is the magic number for this puzzle.

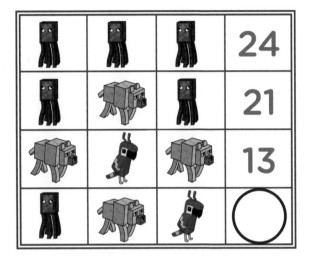

Circle the problems below that have the magic number as their answer. Unscramble those letters to spell the name of a Minecraft mob.

14 +7	17 −6	4 ×4	7 +9	34 −18
A	T	H	O	L

8 ×2	27 −11	4 ×1	12 +4	25 − 9
N	D	R	P	I

—— —— —— —— —— —— ——

A SMASHING SUCCESS

Use the picture-number combination under each blank space to find the correct letter on the grid. The correct letter is the one where the picture and number intersect. If you fill in the spaces correctly, you'll discover a fun tip that can help you be a smashing success!

	🔨	🦴	🐺	🍗
1	T	K	N	A
2	I	U	H	B
3	G	E	R	M
4	C	W	L	O

A player in a minecart on a rail can ride

___ ___ ___ ___ ___ ___ ___
🔨1 🐺2 🐺3 🍗4 🦴2 🔨3 🐺2

−

___ ___ ___ ___ ___ ___ ___ ___
🍗1 🍗4 🐺1 🦴3 🍗2 🐺4 🍗4 🔨4 🦴1

.

___ ___ ___ ___
🦴4 🍗1 🐺4 🐺4

TRUTH BE TOLD

Solve this puzzle and unlock a secret before you're attacked by phantoms! Color every box that has an odd number in it to reveal the word that goes in the blank.

Phantoms were going to be _____,

but designers thought they looked like

Nether mobs.

23	35	18	4	7	39	21	32	13	15	26
17	46	11	28	45	40	12	44	35	48	1
5	43	36	20	29	37	50	2	9	14	21
31	24	27	8	41	16	30	22	35	42	37
49	10	25	38	3	33	47	34	29	45	6

TREAT YOURSELF TO THIS TRICK

Solve the math problems, then use the code-breaker key to treat yourself to a trick you can play on your Minecrafting friends.

32	33	34	35	36	37	38	39	40	41	42	43	44	45	46
A	B	C	D	E	F	G	H	I	J	K	L	M	N	O

47	48	49	50	51	52	53	54	55	56	57
P	Q	R	S	T	U	V	W	X	Y	Z

Do this with ice blocks, slime, or soul sand:

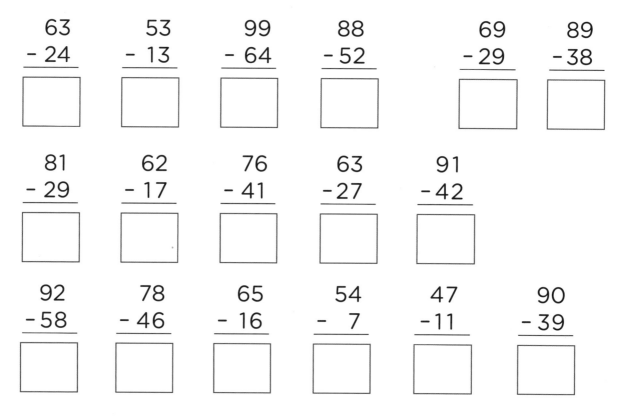

63	53	99	88	69	89
- 24	- 13	- 64	- 52	- 29	- 38

81	62	76	63	91
- 29	- 17	- 41	- 27	- 42

92	78	65	54	47	90
- 58	- 46	- 16	- 7	- 11	- 39

___ ___ ___ ___ ___ ___ ___

___ ___ ___ ___ ___ ___ ___ ___ ___ ___

DON'T LET IT ROLL

The first scale is balanced. The second scale is not, and those spawn eggs are about to roll and start a dangerous chain reaction! How many 🥚 *do you need to balance the second scale? Draw them or write the number on the scale.*

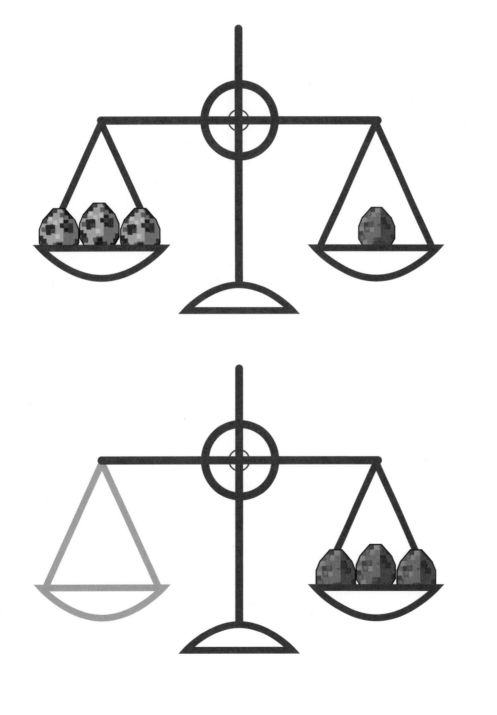

FIRE AWAY

Campfires are useful. Do you know why?

Move from box to box as you count by sixes. Write the letter from each box where you land on the spaces, in order from left to right. Begin with the number 6 and continue until all the spaces are filled. If you count, hop, and copy letters correctly, you'll reveal the one cool thing you can make with a campfire.

27 52		36
L 66	O 18	S (6)
48	42	10
G 34	I 16	N 54
12	30	68
M 37	E 14	K 24
60	26	11
A 20	R 8	D 53

S _ _ _ _ _ _ _ _ _ _

MAGIC NUMBER 11

Have you ever seen this mob spawn naturally?

The numbers at the end of the rows and columns are linked to the images in the grid. What number goes in the circle? This is the magic number for this puzzle.

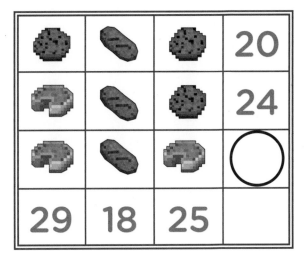

Circle problems below that have the magic number as their answer. Unscramble those letters to spell the name of the Minecraft mob that has a very rare 0.164% chance of spawning naturally.

37 − 9	2 × 14	22 +14	16 +12	21 + 7	84 ÷ 3
I	E	O	H	E	N

41 − 13	35 − 7	56 ÷ 3	17 +11	4 × 7
S	P	N	K	P

____ ____ ____ ____ ____   ____ ____ ____ ____ ____

HERE, BOY

Use the picture-number combination under each missing letter space to find the correct letter on the grid. The correct letter is the one where the picture and number intersect. If you fill in the spaces correctly, you'll discover the answer to the riddle.

Why are illusioners like well-trained dogs?

	🐐	🐟	🦜	🧍
1	G	P	A	S
2	O	F	H	C
3	D	I	E	Z
4	L	M	N	R

They come on

___ ___ ___ ___ ___ ___ ___
2 🐐2 🐟4 🐟4 🦜1 🦜4 🐐3

14

"WE ARE NUMBER 2, HEY!"

Hidden in the grid is a mixed-up mob. It's cheering about being #2. Color every box that has an even number in it, then unscramble the letters to reveal a second-place mob and write it on the line.

74	16	32	49	2	43	98	69	43	80	67	89	28	76	10	58	65	96	38	62
59	4	85	97	90	25	6	37	74	77	26	17	50	51	33	81	9	44	91	19
39	28	73	39	34	16	22	77	62	26	18	99	32	47	6	88	67	6	18	52
75	86	7	55	68	27	38	63	8	93	30	45	16	55	79	74	29	23	11	68
41	54	57	95	72	3	56	25	86	61	44	83	66	84	38	22	35	24	76	94

Unscrambled letters:

___ ___ ___ ___ ___

Do you know in what way this mob comes in second?

_____

STEVE SAYS

Steve has a Minecraft saying that he thinks is super clever. Solve the math problems, then use the code-breaker key to complete Steve's favorite saying.

21	22	23	24	25	26	27	28	29	30	31	32	33	34	35
A	B	C	D	E	F	G	H	I	J	K	L	M	N	O

36	37	38	39	40	41	42	43	44	45	46
P	Q	R	S	T	U	V	W	X	Y	Z

Steve's favorite saying:

3	5	5	8	7	1	15
x 9	x 5	x 7	x 4	x 5	x 27	x 3
27	☐	☐	☐	☐	☐	☐

G __ __ __ __ __ __

rocks, but

3	25	7	27	19	3	6	4	9
x 9	x 1	x 5	x 1	x 2	x 7	x 6	x 7	x 5
☐	☐	☐	☐	☐	☐	☐	☐	☐

__ __ __ __ __ __ __ __ __

is where it's at!

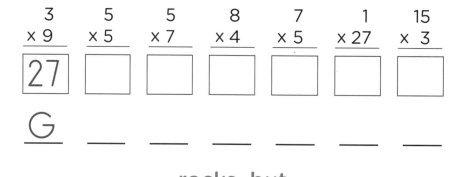

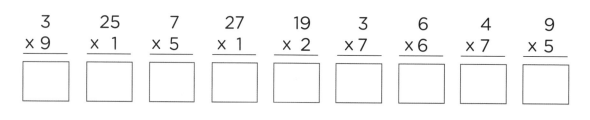

ENDLESS ENCHANTMENTS

The first and second scales are balanced. How many  do you need to balance the third scale? Draw them or write the number on the scale. If you balance the scale correctly, you will be able to enchant every item in your inventory!

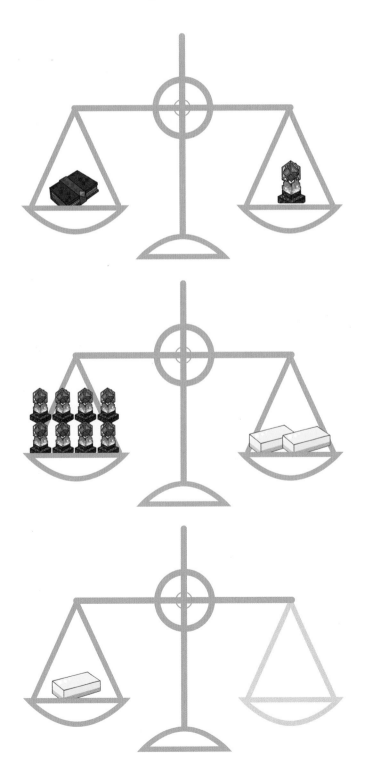

FIRE POWER

Move from box to box as you count by threes. Write the letter from each box where you land on the spaces, in order from left to right. Begin with the number 3 and continue until all the spaces are filled. If you count, hop, and copy letters correctly, you'll fill in the blank below.

A crossbow loaded with fireworks will

damage _____, even at long range.

30 M 15 R 18	25	21 E 19
23 U 12 E 13	(3)	6 N 24
28 C 16	9 D 27	8 P 22

E _ _ _ _ _ _ _

MAGIC NUMBER III

If you fail to solve this puzzle, your ship is sunk!

The numbers at the end of the rows and columns are linked to the images in the grid. What number goes in the circle? This is the magic number for this puzzle.

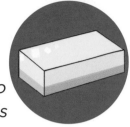

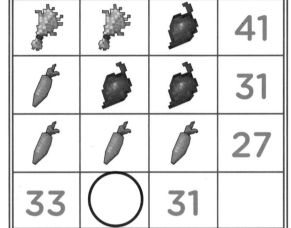

Circle the problems below that have the magic number as their answer. Unscramble those letters to spell the answer to the joke.

Why did the Nitwit sink the boat with too much iron, gold, and redstone?

19 +16	5 ×7	4 ×8	47 −12	57 −22	49 − 7
E	N	J	O	S	G

28 + 7	32 + 3	41 − 6	6 ×2	7 ×5	21 +14
D	A	E	K	I	R

Because he heard the captain say,

" _____ "

___ ___ ___ ___   ___ ___ ___ ___ ___ ___.

SPUH-LASH

Splash texts are the yellow lines of text on the title screen. They might be inside jokes, bits of advice, or nonsense.

Use the picture-number combination under each missing letter space to find the correct letter on the grid. The correct letter is the one where the picture and number intersect. If you fill in the spaces correctly, you'll discover splash text that's also a useful piece of Minecraft advice.

1	G	V	E	U
2	A	P	O	D
3	R	I	H	W
4	Z	C	N	T

HUNT AND FIND

Color every box that has a multiple of 2 in it to discover what's hidden in the grid. There's loot in it for you, if you can find it.

24	86	12	10	58
68	51	17	25	44
1	70	94	36	73
23	81	35	47	13
26	82	54	18	4
48	95	41	5	33
62	22	34	72	20
9	69	15	21	51
16	40	6	76	94
11	37	19	28	7
31	43	82	61	53
36	50	66	18	70
55	3	45	21	59
2	88	46	72	98
54	25	79	19	26
90	71	94	89	38
38	42	6	83	14
57	93	59	37	53
64	10	78	94	26
54	75	62	29	72
26	39	85	1	34
13	27	65	61	11
74	16	28	50	74
68	39	15	97	92
24	52	60	78	30
87	31	23	99	67
18	34	62	90	58
43	9	55	22	41
17	35	30	57	3
96	68	42	56	74

What? You can't read it? Try turning the page on its side.

INSIDE RIDDLE

The letters in the code-breaker key spell the answers to both riddles below. Solve the math problems to decipher the answer to the first riddle. Then cross off those letters inside the code-breaker key to reveal the answer to the second riddle.

What large object sometimes generates on a beach?

13	14	15	16	17	18	19	20	21	22	23	24	25	26	27	28
I	S	H	C	I	E	P	W	B	R	E	E	R	C	K	G

12
+ 2
[14]

31
− 16
[ ]

6
+ 11
[ ]

27
− 8
[ ]

5
× 4
[ ]

17
+ 5
[ ]

6
× 4
[ ]

34
− 8
[ ]

9
× 3
[ ]

S __ __ __ __ __ __ __ __

Where else does it generate?

__ __ __ __ __ __ __ __

UNDER PRESSURE

The first and second scales are balanced. How many 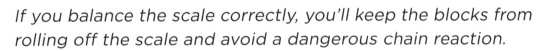 do you need to balance the third scale? Draw them or write the number on the scale.

If you balance the scale correctly, you'll keep the blocks from rolling off the scale and avoid a dangerous chain reaction.

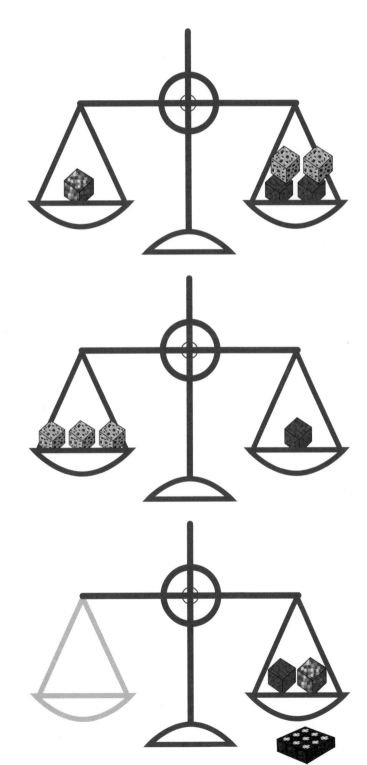

JUMP FIVE

Beginning with the number 19, jump from box to box by adding 5 each time you move. Write the letter from each box where you land on the blank letter spaces, in order from left to right. You'll reveal a Minecraft game where players jump around.

29	59	39
R	N	O
49	28	79
44	40 · 45	
U	E	A
35	64	24
29	9	8
P	K	L
(19)	34	22

P _ _ _ _ _ _

24

MAGIC NUMBER IV

The numbers at the end of the rows are linked to the images in the grid. What number goes in the circle? This is the magic number.

Circle the problems below that have the magic number as their answer. Unscramble those letters to spell the name of a Minecraft mob.

28 + 2	6 x 5	26 + 4	33 - 22	17 +24	15 x 2
N	L	G	I	R	E
21 +9	51 -11	16 +14	76 -46	53 -23	42 -12
W	C	O	M	S	O

__ __ __ __ __ __ __ __ __

SLOW GOING

Cobwebs are great for slowing down mobs and arrows, but they have another clever use, too.

Use the picture-number combination under each blank letter space to find the correct letter on the grid. The correct letter is the one where the picture and number intersect. If you fill in the spaces correctly, you'll discover another fun use for cobwebs.

Use cobwebs to create delays in _____.

	🍪	💎	🥚	🌼
1	D	A	T	N
2	U	B	K	R
3	O	C	S	G
4	W	E	L	I

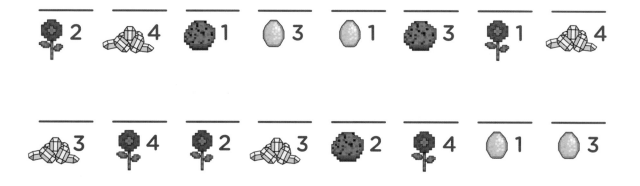

A SPILLED SECRET

It's more of a cure than a secret, really, but you still don't want to spill it.

Color every box that has a multiple of 3 in it to reveal this handy item.

78	84	22	30	18	65	6	16	75	49	69	20	53	99
36	17	60	43	45	70	41	35	90	4	33	64	42	58
57	14	51	65	24	88	42	50	27	31	51	96	56	44
21	2	28	91	33	61	54	11	63	73	45	62	39	27
45	37	19	8	42	7	15	26	48	56	60	7	22	75

 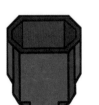 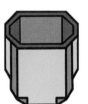 

ALERT! ALERT! ALERT!

Use this handy trick to stay safe when you're working in your Minecraft house . . . or office . . . or lab . . . or anywhere indoors.

Solve the math problems, then use the code-breaker key to reveal this useful tip.

14	15	16	17	18	19	20	21	22	23	24	25	26	27	28
A	B	C	D	E	F	G	H	I	J	K	L	M	N	O

29	30	31	32	33	34	35	36	37	38	39
P	Q	R	S	T	U	V	W	X	Y	Z

If you want to hear when hostile mobs are approaching, surround your building with

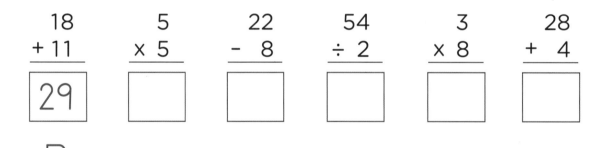

$$18 + 11 \qquad 5 \times 5 \qquad 22 - 8 \qquad 54 \div 2 \qquad 3 \times 8 \qquad 28 + 4$$

29

P ___ ___ ___ ___ ___ .

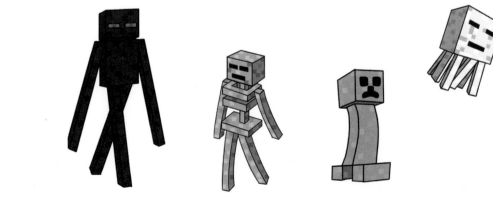

A BALANCED DIET

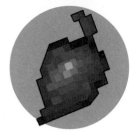

You've gotta eat to survive!

The first and second scales are balanced. How many 🥩 do you need to balance the third scale? Draw them or write the number on the scale.

If you balance the scale correctly, you will refill your hunger bar.

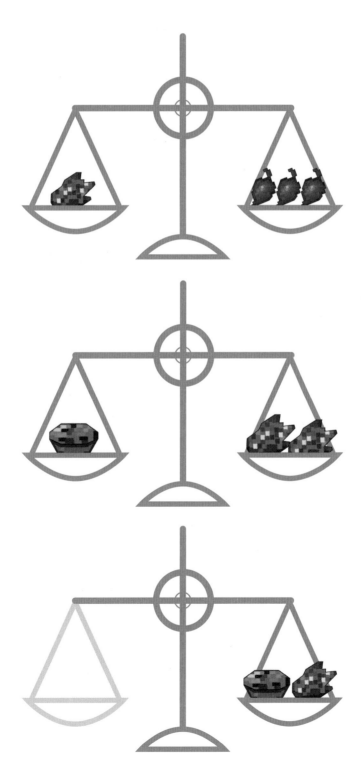

TWINZIES

Beginning with the number 75, count up by fives. Write the letter from each box where you land on the spaces, in order from left to right until all spaces are filled.

If you count, hop, and copy letters correctly, you'll reveal the answer to this question:

What do you call Alex's zombie twin?

84	115	93	100
E	G	O	R
120	96	145 125	125
130	82	(75)	111
X	I	A	E
99	105	90	85
101	95	106	79
O	D	C	N
135	80	140	110

A _ _ _ _ _ _ _

_ _ _ _ _ _

The numbers at the end of the rows are linked to the images in the grid. What number goes in the circle? This is the magic number for this puzzle.

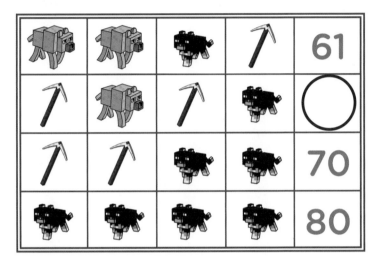

				61
				⃝
				70
				80

Circle the problems below that have the magic number as their answer. Unscramble those letters to reveal a play mode that gives you more control over the Minecraft world.

76 -13	8 x7	45 + 2	7 x9	91 -28
F	N	A	U	F

98 -34	47 +16	84 -19	21 x 3	28 +35
G	B	B	E	T

__ __ __ __ __ __ __

LOOKING UP

Have you ever gotten lost in Minecraft? Use the picture-number combination under each blank letter space to find the correct letter on the grid. The correct letter is the one where the picture and number intersect. If you fill in the spaces correctly, you'll discover a unique method for finding your way in Minecraft.

1	O	A	T	H
2	Y	P	E	M
3	B	K	W	R
4	L	V	X	S

Watch the sun, moon, stars, and clouds, because they

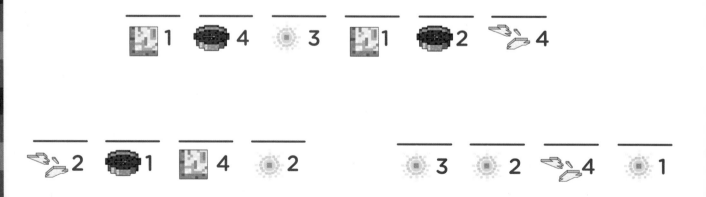

32

GET SOME PERSPECTIVE

Color every box that has a multiple of 5 to reveal the key on your keyboard that changes your view in the game from first person to third person. Hint: *The answer lies in the uncolored squares.*

What is the key? _____

14	58	22	30	17	63	92
39	75	15	50	87	20	45
66	4	60	25	51	42	6
48	80	5	40	35	10	27
52	65	70	55	11	49	88

33

WHAT IS THE MEANING OF THIS?

Solve the math problems, then use the code-breaker key to reveal a fun fact about the company that makes Minecraft.

48	49	50	51	52	53	54	55	56	57	58	59	60	61	62
A	B	C	D	E	F	G	H	I	J	K	L	M	N	O

63	64	65	66	67	68	69	70	71	72	73
P	Q	R	S	T	U	V	W	X	Y	Z

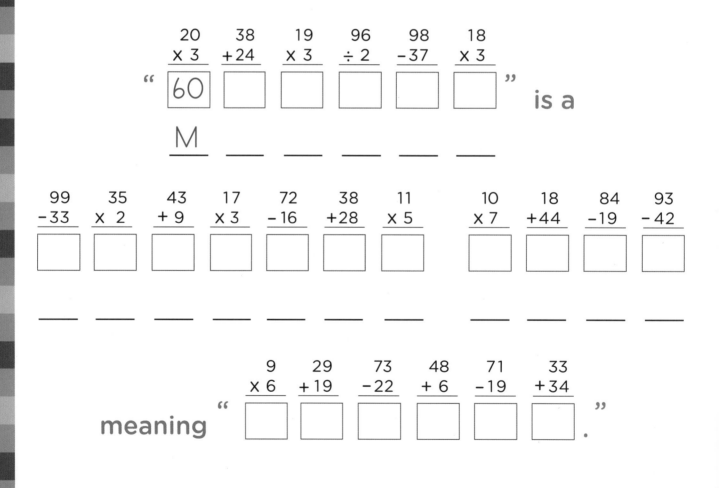

$$20 \times 3 \qquad 38 + 24 \qquad 19 \times 3 \qquad 96 \div 2 \qquad 98 - 37 \qquad 18 \times 3$$

" 60 ☐ ☐ ☐ ☐ ☐ " is a

M __ __ __ __ __

$$99 - 33 \quad 35 \times 2 \quad 43 + 9 \quad 17 \times 3 \quad 72 - 16 \quad 38 + 28 \quad 11 \times 5 \qquad 10 \times 7 \quad 18 + 44 \quad 84 - 19 \quad 93 - 42$$

☐ ☐ ☐ ☐ ☐ ☐ ☐   ☐ ☐ ☐ ☐

__ __ __ __ __ __ __   __ __ __ __

$$9 \times 6 \qquad 29 + 19 \qquad 73 - 22 \qquad 48 + 6 \qquad 71 - 19 \qquad 33 + 34$$

meaning " ☐ ☐ ☐ ☐ ☐ ☐ " .

__ __ __ __ __ __

PAYMENT BALANCE

Villagers insist you balance the payment scales below. If you don't, they vow to pillage your inventory.

The first and second scales are balanced. How many 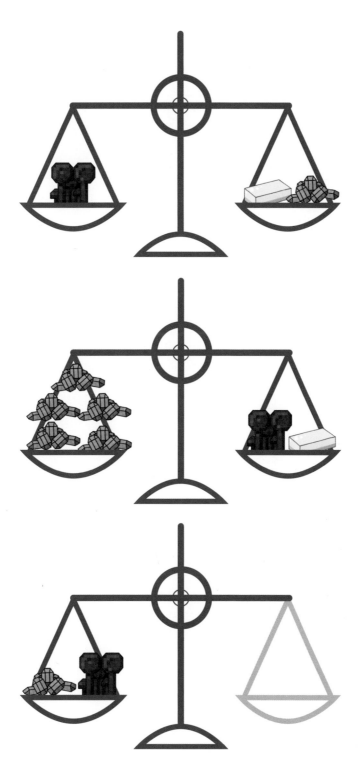 do you need to balance the third scale? Draw them or write the number on the scale.

MAGIC NUMBER VI

The numbers at the end of the rows and columns are linked to the images in the grid. What number goes in the circle? This is the magic number for this puzzle.

				42
				84
				◯
				47
39	55	64	67	

Circle the problems below that have the magic number as their answer. Unscramble those letters to reveal a clever way to locate hidden caves.

79 −25	13 ×4	64 −12	18 × 3	8 × 6	25 +27
E	O	S	A	D	P

78 −26	41 + 2	13 +39	26 × 2	80 +24
I	B	T	N	C

___ ___ ___ ___ ___ ___

PRO BUILDER TIP

Design and build cool structures and scenes with this pro tip.

Use the picture-number combination under each blank letter space to find the correct letter on the grid. The correct letter is the one where the picture and number intersect. If you fill in the spaces correctly, you'll discover a unique method for crafting amazing buildings and landscapes.

1	I	T	L	R
2	W	E	U	A
3	N	Q	S	H
4	M	G	V	D

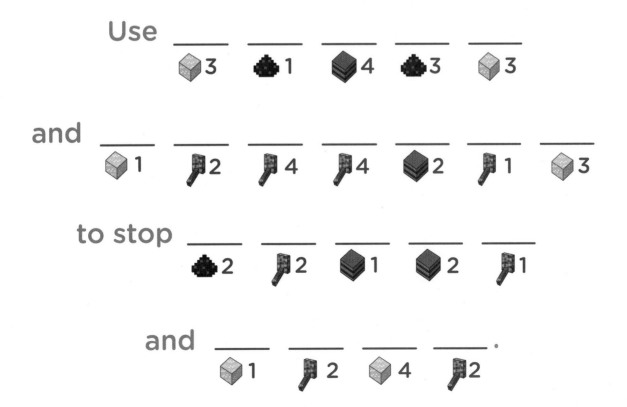

Use ___ ___ ___ ___ ___
(🔲3 🔵1 ⬛4 🔵3 🔲3)

and ___ ___ ___ ___ ___ ___ ___
(🔲1 2 4 4 ⬛2 1 🔲3)

to stop ___ ___ ___ ___ ___
(🔵2 2 ⬛1 ⬛2 1)

and ___ ___ ___ ___.
(🔲1 2 🔲4 2)

37

HIDDEN RESOURCE

Color every box with a number that is divisible by 3. If you color the boxes correctly, you'll shed some light on a useful Minecraft item.

33	15	81	86	75	39	24	70	66	30	72	11	72	3	18	34	75	19	87
8	90	76	35	42	89	51	43	93	91	87	82	36	55	96	74	99	61	57
26	48	41	20	96	14	78	1	6	12	54	2	21	59	79	25	15	60	24
77	63	67	47	36	83	45	88	54	81	32	65	9	17	42	68	51	80	39
49	9	22	40	21	69	18	71	84	94	90	85	48	66	84	46	78	13	45

NEIGHM YOUR HORSE

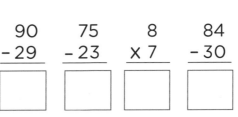

Is there such a thing as too many Minecraft jokes? Neigh!

Find the sums of the math problems, then use the code-breaker key to decipher the punchline of this joke.

48	49	50	51	52	53	54	55	56	57	58	59	60	61	62
A	B	C	D	E	F	G	H	I	J	K	L	M	N	O

63	64	65	66	67	68	69	70	71	72	73
P	Q	R	S	T	U	V	W	X	Y	Z

Alex calls her horse "Mayo," and

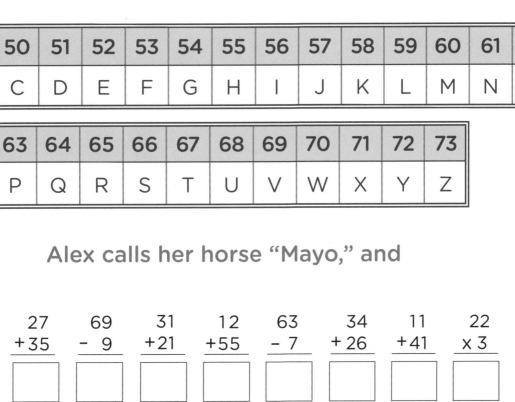

54 +12	27 +35	69 − 9	31 +21	12 +55	63 − 7	34 +26	11 +41	22 × 3
66								
S								

31 +29	64 −16	31 +41	31 × 2	90 −29	75 −23	8 × 7	84 −30	72 −17	11 × 6

THE POINT IS... SHARP!

The first and second scales are balanced. How many  do you need to balance the third scale? Draw them or write the number on the scale before the cactus rolls and you feel its spikes. Ouch!

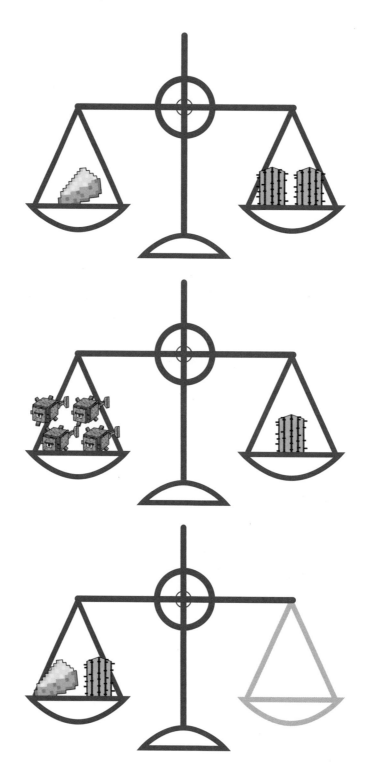

ASK AND RECEIVE

Hop from box to box counting by sevens. Write the letter from each box where you land on the spaces, in order from left to right, until all spaces are filled.

If you count, hop, and copy letters correctly, you'll reveal the decorative item that was added at the suggestion of a Minecraft fan like you.

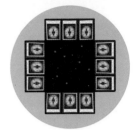

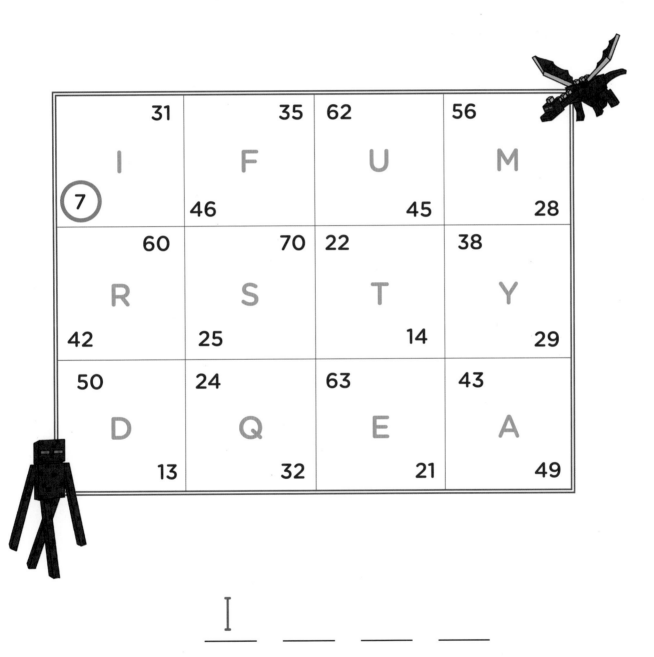

31	35	62	56
I	F	U	M
⑦	46	45	28
60	70 22		38
R	S	T	Y
42	25	14	29
50	24	63	43
D	Q	E	A
13	32	21	49

I __ __ __

__ __ __ __ __ __

MAGIC NUMBER VII

The numbers at the end of the rows and columns are linked to the images in the grid. What number goes in the circle? This is the magic number for this puzzle.

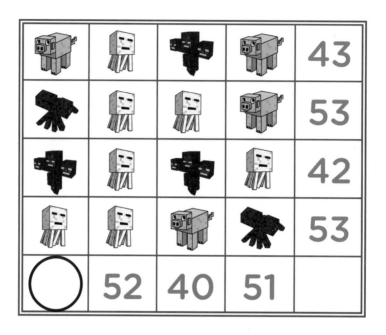

Circle the problems below that have the magic number as their answer. Unscramble those letters to spell the name of a Minecraft mob.

6	17	2	57	7	36
x 8	+31	x 24	− 9	x 7	+13
S	**I**	**H**	**L**	**A**	**B**

60	12	33	4	16	29
−12	x 4	+15	x 12	x 3	+19
R	**S**	**V**	**F**	**E**	**I**

___ ___ ___ ___ ___ ___ ___

ZOMBIE-PROOF

Use the picture-number combination under each space to find the correct letter on the grid. The correct letter is the one where the picture and number intersect. If you fill in the spaces correctly, you'll discover a useful Minecraft tip for protecting yourself from zombies.

	🐺	🧊	🥕	🥔
1	O	V	C	I
2	B	S	L	D
3	F	G	R	M
4	J	N	A	E

Want to zombie-proof your castle?

___ 3 ___ 4 ___ 4 ___ 1 ___ 4 ___ 2

make excellent

___ 2 ___ 1 ___ 1 ___ 3 ___ 2

43

A MINECRAFT CHALLENGE

Solve this puzzle to reveal a particular kind of Minecraft challenge! Color every box with a number that is divisible by 4.

92	32	60	14	96	12	68	58	8	38	22	54	96
56	34	4	22	78	44	18	70	64	28	10	24	48
24	62	14	30	38	84	42	46	88	72	36	56	52
80	94	48	74	66	52	10	82	40	98	92	26	16
36	72	16	50	18	20	34	26	76	90	86	42	68

HIDDEN PASSAGE

Use your math skills to crack the code. Solve the math problems and use the code-breaker key to find the letters that spell out where you can find a hidden passage.

9	10	11	12	13	14	15	16	17	18
S	E	T	N	R	D	O	P	N	O

19	20	21	22	23	24	25	26	27
G	R	H	T	O	A	L	L	D

3	45	7	24	15	12	3	31	5	19
× 3	−34	+ 6	− 9	+ 2	+ 7	× 7	− 8	× 5	+ 8

Now, cross out the letters you used in the code-breaker key and write the remaining letters in order on the space below.

What is the hidden passage called?

_____

YOUR FATE, IN THE BALANCE

As long as the scales are balanced, you are safe. As soon as one tips, even the slightest bit, you're a goner. The first and second scales are balanced. How many 🧟 do you need to balance the third scale? Draw them or write the number on the scale before the lava or the husks destroy you!

A NETHER JOKE

Beginning with the number 14, move from box to box by adding 3 each time you move. Write the letter from each box where you land on the spaces, in order from left to right, until all spaces are filled. If you count, hop, and copy letters correctly, you'll reveal the punchline to this joke:

Did you hear about the Minecraft player who went to sleep in the Nether?

20 C	50 E	23 A	53 N
11	29	38 46	46
35 O	(14) H	22 A	32 T
59	55	33	51
26 M	47 D	17 E	8 B
37	56	44	41

H __ __   __ __ __ __   __ __   __   __ __ __   __ __ __ __

__ __ __ __ __   __ __ __!

MAGIC NUMBER VIII

The numbers at the end of the rows and columns are linked to the images in the grid. What number goes in the circle? This is the magic number for this puzzle.

				43
				34
				38
				◯
50	33	48	24	

Circle the problems below that have the magic number as their answer. Unscramble those letters to spell the name of a new, underwater block that can be activated to attack hostile mobs.

8 x 5	18 +13	26 +14	48 - 8	4 x 10
D	E	I	U	C

57 -17	2 x20	47 - 9	62 x 2	27 +13
N	T	L	S	O

_ _ _ _ _ _ _

AIM HIGH

Reaching higher altitudes is possible only if you know this trick. Use the picture-number combination under each blank letter space to find the correct letter on the grid. The correct letter is the one where the picture and number intersect. If you fill in the spaces correctly, you'll discover a useful Minecraft skill.

	🦜	▦	➤	🐉
1	L	N	E	J
2	C	U	P	G
3	I	S	T	R
4	O	A	M	K

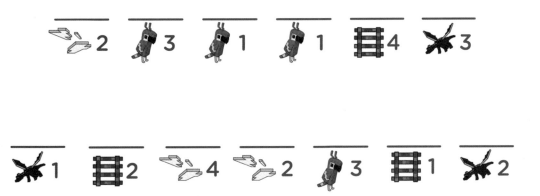

MINECRAFT LINGO

Are you up on Minecraft lingo? Color every box that contains a multiple of 7. If you color the boxes correctly, you'll reveal a term that competitive Minecrafters know.

37	54	77	47	38	84	32	94	60	81	42
64	50	35	92	28	61	14	37	45	34	91
70	14	63	59	56	43	77	65	98	42	56
84	73	7	31	42	72	63	52	35	86	49
98	21	49	87	91	36	14	46	70	28	7

Wait a minute, that's not right! Try turning the book upside down to read the term for competitive gaming.

A DIFFERENT POV

Solve the math problems, then use the code-breaker key to figure out which option in Minecraft allows you to turn everything black and white or upside down.

37	38	39	40	41	42	43	44	45	46	47	48	49	50	51
A	B	C	D	E	F	G	H	I	J	K	L	M	N	O

52	53	54	55	56	57	58	59	60	61	62
P	Q	R	S	T	U	V	W	X	Y	Z

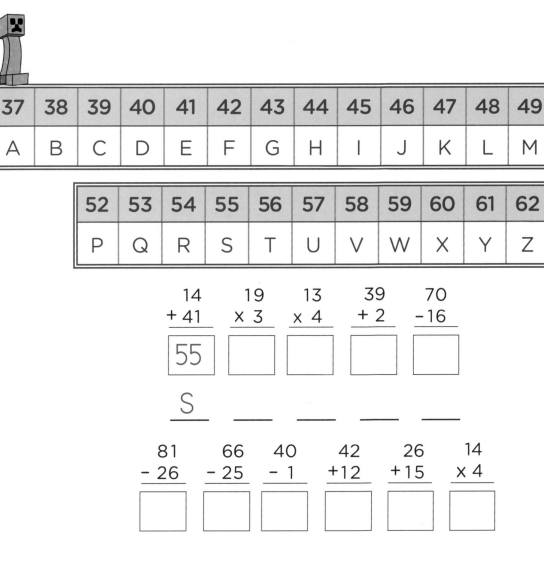

14 + 41	19 × 3	13 × 4	39 + 2	70 −16
55				

S __ __ __ __

81 − 26	66 − 25	40 − 1	42 +12	26 +15	14 × 4

__ __ __ __ __ __

37 +18	80 − 39	67 − 11	48 + 8	9 × 5	77 − 27	27 +16	72 − 17

__ __ __ __ __ __ __ __

A SLIMING SCALE

The first and second scales are balanced. How many  do you need to balance the third scale? Draw them or write the number on the scale. If you balance the scale correctly, you get to keep the redstone.

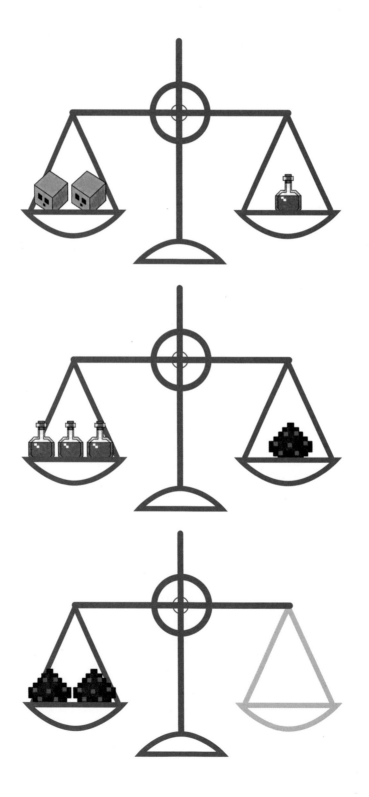

MINING SHORTCUT

This shortcut can save you tons of time. Beginning with the number 22, move from box to box by adding 4 each time you move. Write the letter from each box where you land on the spaces, in order from left to right, until all spaces are filled. If you count, hop, and copy letters correctly, you'll reveal a time-saving mining technique.

30	86	78	82
N	S	H	E
84	(22)	56	54
25	58	42	34
I	L	R	D
72	32	70	40
66	92	52	88
O	G	Y	T
90	38	60	62
50	80	46	74
V	F	A	C
94	76	26	64

Mine S __ __ __ and __ __ __ __ __ __

with __ __ __ __ __ __ __ .

FALL FIX

Have you ever been destroyed in the game by a bad fall? Next time, use this to survive. Solve the math problems, then use the code-breaker key to reveal a handy tip for avoiding falls.

45	46	47	48	49	50	51	52	53	54	55	56	57	58	59
A	B	C	D	E	F	G	H	I	J	K	L	M	N	O

60	61	62	63	64	65	66	67	68	69	70
P	Q	R	S	T	U	V	W	X	Y	Z

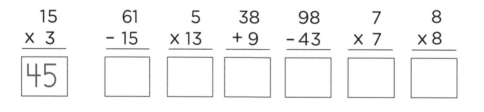

15	61	5	38	98	7	8
x 3	− 15	x 13	+ 9	− 43	x 7	x 8
45						

A __ __ __ __ __ __

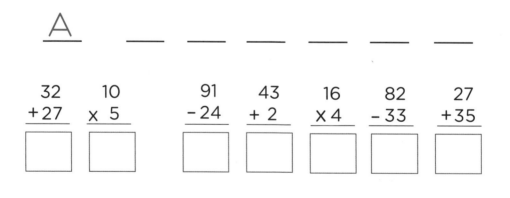

32	10		91	43	16	82	27
+ 27	x 5		− 24	+ 2	x 4	− 33	+ 35

__ __ __ __ __ __ __

BALANCE OF NATURE

Can you preserve the delicate balance of nature? The first and second scales are balanced. How many  do you need to balance the third scale? Draw them or write the number on the scale.

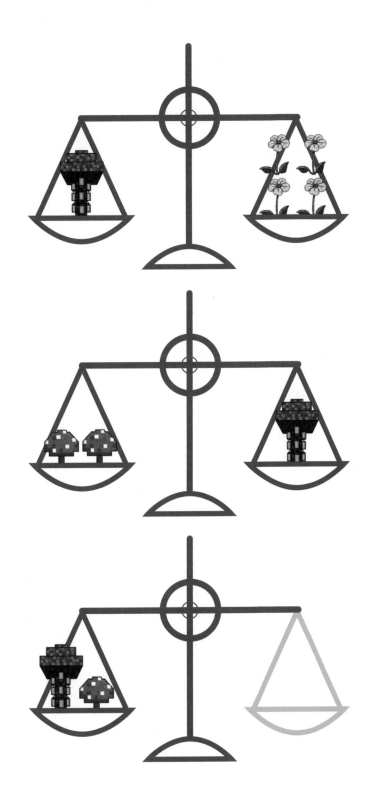

MAGIC NUMBER IX

The numbers at the end of the rows and columns are linked to the images in the grid. What number goes in the circle? This is the magic number for this puzzle.

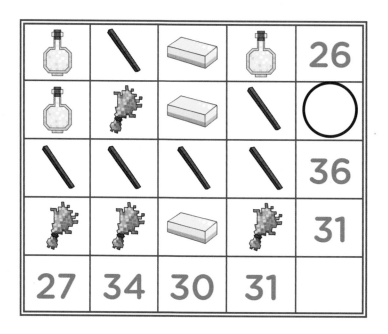

Write the magic number on the left-most line below. Subtract 25 from this magic number to find out how many chicks can spawn from one Minecraft chicken egg.

_____ – 25 = _____ chicks

ANSWERS

PAGE 4
A PRICKLY SUBJECT
A PORKYSPINE

PAGE 5
IN THE BALANCE
4 experience orbs

PAGE 6
HILARIOUS HAUNT
ZOMBEAGLE

PAGE 7
MAGIC NUMBER 1
16 - DOLPHIN

PAGE 8
A SMASHING SUCCESS
A player in a minecart on a rail can ride
THROUGH A ONE-BLOCK WALL

PAGE 9
TRUTH BE TOLD

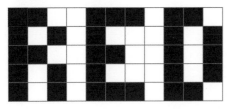

PAGE 10
TREAT YOURSELF TO THIS TRICK
Do this with ice blocks, slime, or soul
sand: HIDE IT UNDER CARPET.
Friends won't see it, but the effects
will still work, so they'll slip, bounce,
or slooooooow down.

PAGE 11
DON'T LET IT ROLL
9 zombie pigman spawn eggs

PAGE 12
FIRE AWAY
SMOKE SIGNAL

PAGE 13
MAGIC NUMBER 11
28 - PINK SHEEP

PAGE 14
HERE, BOY
They come on COMMAND.
Get it? Illusioners don't spawn naturally, but
you can make them spawn with the /summon
illusioner command.

PAGE 15
"WE ARE NUMBER 2, HEY!"

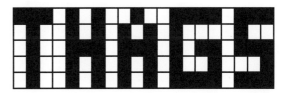

The mob is the GHAST, and it is the second
largest mob in Minecraft. The Ender Dragon
is largest.

PAGE 16
STEVE SAYS
GEOLOGY rocks, but GEOGRAPHY is
where it's at!

PAGE 17
ENDLESS ENCHANTMENTS
4 enchanted books

PAGE 18
FIRE POWER
ENDERMEN

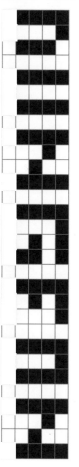
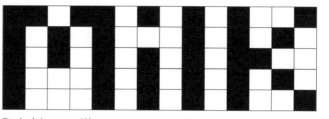

PAGE 31
MAGIC NUMBER V

63 - BUFFET
You choose how a Buffet world is
customized.

PAGE 32
LOOKING UP

ALWAYS MOVE WEST

PAGE 33
GET SOME PERSPECTIVE

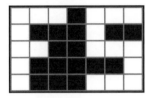

F5 shows up in the negative space of this
puzzle. It is a function key on a keyboard,
and it's used to change the player's per-
spective. For instance, you can see the
back of your head or even your face as
you play the game.

PAGE 34
WHAT IS THE MEANING OF THIS?

"MOJANG" is a SWEDISH WORD
meaning "GADGET."
Mojang (pronounced "mo-YANG") is
the name of the company that makes
Minecraft.

PAGE 35
PAYMENT BALANCE

2 gold ingots

PAGE 36
MAGIC NUMBER VI

52 - PISTON
A piston can be placed against a wall
where you think a cave is hiding. If it
pushes out, that means there might be
a cave within 12 blocks. Dig for it!

PAGE 37
PRO BUILDER TIP

Use SIGNS and LADDERS to stop WATER
and LAVA.

PAGE 38
HIDDEN RESOURCE

PAGE 39
NEIGHM YOUR HORSE

Alex calls her horse "Mayo," and SOME-
TIMES MAYO NEIGHS!

PAGE 40
THE POINT IS . . . SHARP!

12 guardians

PAGE 41
ASK AND RECEIVE

ITEM FRAMES

PAGE 42
MAGIC NUMBER VII

48 - SILVERFISH

PAGE 43
ZOMBIE-PROOF

FENCES make excellent DOORS. Zombies can't break the fences, and you can fight back through the fences. Genius!

PAGE 44
A MINECRAFT CHALLENGE

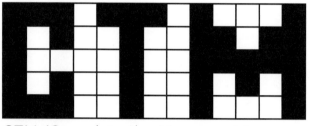

CTM (Complete the Monument.)

PAGE 45
HIDDEN PASSAGE

STRONGHOLD
END PORTAL

PAGE 46
YOUR FATE, IN THE BALANCE

9 creepers

PAGE 47
A NETHER JOKE

Did you hear about the Minecraft player who went to sleep in the Nether? HE CAME TO A BED END.

PAGE 48
MAGIC NUMBER VIII

40 - CONDUIT

PAGE 49
AIM HIGH

PILLAR JUMPING - The pillar is placed while you're jumping.

PAGE 50
MINECRAFT LINGO

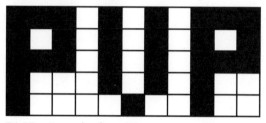

PVP stands for Player vs. Player.

PAGE 51
A DIFFERENT POV

SUPER SECRET SETTINGS

PAGE 52
A SLIMING SCALE

12 slime blocks

PAGE 53
MINING SHORTCUT

Mine SAND and GRAVEL with TORCHES.

PAGE 54
FALL FIX

A BUCKET OF WATER

PAGE 55
BALANCE OF NATURE

6 flowers

PAGE 56
MAGIC NUMBER IX

29 - 4 chicks

CERTIFICATE OF ACHIEVEMENT
CONGRATULATIONS

This certifies that

_____

Name

became a

MINECRAFT PUZZLE BOSS

on _____.

Date

_____

Signature

ALSO AVAILABLE

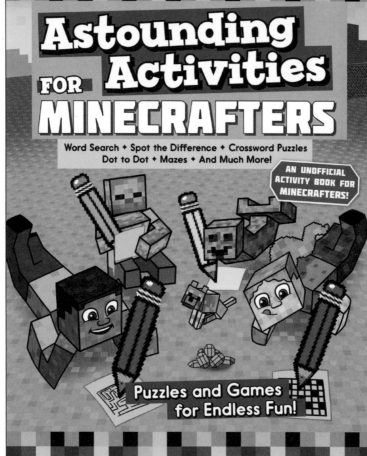